Kid's Box

New Generation

British English

Caroline Nixon &
Michael Tomlinson

CAMBRIDGE

Activity Book
with Digital Pack

2

Thanks and Acknowledgements

Authors' thanks

Many thanks to everyone at Cambridge University Press for their dedication and hard work, and in particular to:

Liane Grainger and Lynn Townsend for supervising the whole project and guiding us calmly through the storms;

Alison Bewsher for her keen editorial eye, enthusiasm and great suggestions;

Amy Few and Liz Wilkie for their hard work, enthusiasm, and good ideas.

We would also like to thank all our pupils and colleagues, past, present and future, at Star English academy in Murcia, especially Jim Kelly for his friendship and support throughout the years.

Dedications

For my dearest sisters, Elaine and Teresa. We are Family. – CN

For my great friends in England, who always receive us so kindly, offering their warmth and friendship: Mike and Nicola, and Shaun and Lorraine. – MT

The authors and publishers acknowledge the following sources of copyright material and are grateful for the permissions granted. While every effort has been made, it has not always been possible to identify the sources of all the material used, or to trace all copyright holders. If any omissions are brought to our notice, we will be happy to include the appropriate acknowledgements on reprinting and in the next update to the digital edition, as applicable.

Key: U = Unit

Photography

The following photos are sourced from Getty Images.

U2: dejan Jekic/iStock/Getty Images Plus; aopsan/iStock/Getty Images Plus; Inna Mykhalchuk/iStock/Getty Images Plus; Vyacheslav Petelin/iStock/Getty Images Plus; WLADIMIR BULGAR/SCIENCE PHOTO LIBRARY/Science Photo Library; Jose Luis Pelaez Inc/DigitalVision; t_kimura/E+; rclassenlayouts/iStock/Getty Images Plus; Thomas Söllner/EyeEm; dsafanda/iStock/Getty Images Plus; Peerasak Kamngoen/EyeEm; Sergey05/iStock/Getty Images Plus; BraunS/E+; mediaphotos/E+; monkeybusinessimages/iStock/Getty Images Plus; Fotosearch; alvarez/E+; **U4:** Floresco Productions/OJO Images; Elena María Sánchez/EyeEm; Aslan Alphan/E+; cavemanboon/Moment; Tahreer Photography/Moment; jayk7/Moment; FotografiaBasica/E+; belchonock; Arina_Bogachyova/iStock/Getty Images Plus; lucas1958/iStock/Getty Images Plus; omersukrugoksu/E+; kali9/E+; Comstock Images/Stockbyte; JGI/Jamie Grill; Silke Enkelmann/EyeEm; Garry518/iStock/Getty Images Plus; sqback/iStock/Getty Images Plus; Kseniya Ovchinnikova/Moment; CSA Images; gerenme/iStock/Getty Images Plus; Pieter Estersohn/Corbis Documentary; **U6:** Nang Saw Thay Y Laksn Chun Vthay/EyeEm; Jaswinder Singh/iStock/Getty Images Plus; Xinzheng/Moment; jlvphoto/iStock/Getty Images Plus; atoss/iStock/Getty Images Plus; Yevgen Romanenko/Moment; IvonneW/iStock/Getty Images Plus; verdateo/iStock/Getty Images Plus; Paul Poplis/Photolibrary/Getty Images Plus; ChoochartSansong/iStock/Getty Images Plus; Tung-Tong/iStock/Getty Images Plus; chengyuzheng/iStock/Getty Images Plus; lunglee/iStock/Getty Images Plus; Chaiwat Hemakom/iStock/Getty Images Plus; chengyuzheng/iStock/Getty Images Plus; MirageC/Moment; malerapaso/iStock/Getty Images Plus; kbwills/iStock/Getty Images Plus; AndreyGorulko/iStock/Getty Images Plus; ttatty/iStock/Getty Images Plus; MediaProduction/iStock/Getty Images Plus; Magone/iStock/Getty Images Plus; robertsre/iStock/Getty Images Plus; talevr/iStock/Getty Images Plus; Visoot Uthairam/EyeEm; Lorna Rande/Design Pics; Sergio Amiti/Moment; jxfzsy/E+; JoeGough/iStock/Getty Images Plus; kivoart/E+; Luc TEBOUL/Moment; travellinglight/iStock/Getty Images Plus; Robert Morrissey/EyeEm; Westend61; Wisan Tangphoo/EyeEm; Simone_Capozzi/iStock/Getty Images Plus; Irina_Strelnikova/iStock/Getty Images Plus; **U7:** GlobalP/iStock/Getty Images Plus; MirekKijewski/iStock/Getty Images Plus; DaydreamsGirl/E+; Andrew_Howe/E+; kerkla/E+; Elena Levchenko/EyeEm; Nicholas Cope/DigitalVision; Natthawut Nungsanther/EyeEm; GK Hart/Vikki Hart/Photodisc; Andyworks/E+; Fuse/Corbis; Digital Zoo/Photodisc; **U8:** John D. Buffington/DigitalVision; Benjamin Rondel/The Image Bank; Peter Cade/The Image Bank Unreleased; Lisa Bennett/EyeEm; Layland Masuda/Moment; peterspiro/iStock/Getty Images Plus; kodachrome25/iStock/Getty Images Plus;

LIU KAIYOU/Moment; Eri Morita/Photodisc; MarioGuti/iStock/Getty Images Plus; Enis Aksoy/DigitalVision Vectors; fonikum/DigitalVision Vectors; CSA Images; rambo182/DigitalVision Vectors; -VICTOR-/DigitalVision Vectors; LueratSatichob/DigitalVision Vectors; appleuzr/DigitalVision Vectors; Steppeua/DigitalVision Vectors; alexialex/iStock/Getty Images Plus; Anton Eine/EyeEm; Jake Wyman/The Image Bank; CoffmanCMU/iStock/Getty Images Plus; Charles Bowman/Photolibrary/Getty Images Plus; kali9/E+; izabell-/iStock/Getty Images Plus; **U9:** Nina Erhart/EyeEm; Ng Sok Lian/EyeEm; C Squared Studios/Photodisc; PhotoAlto/Frederic Cirou/PhotoAlto Agency RF Collections; hudiemm/E+; istanbulimage/E+; Red Sky/Moment; rusm/E+; Westend61; Creative Crop/DigitalVision; tunart/E+; Juanmonino/iStock/Getty Images Plus; Jose Luis Pelaez Inc/DigitalVision; **U10:** Michael Burrell/iStock/Getty Images Plus; pepifoto/iStock/Getty Images Plus; skodonnell/iStock/Getty Images Plus; mladn61/iStock/Getty Images Plus; sihuo0860371/iStock/Getty Images Plus; Thomas Northcut/Photodisc; Daniel Milchev/The Image Bank; Stephen Frink/The Image Bank; Adam Gault/Photographer's Choice RF; Oliver Rossi/Stone; Patrik Giardino/Stone; Clover No.7 Photography/Moment; PeopleImages/iStock/Getty Images Plus; Image Source/Photodisc; Yoshiyoshi Hirokawa/DigitalVision; Marc Dufresne/E+; **U11:** Radionphoto/iStock/Getty Images Plus; ALAMA/iStock/Getty Images Plus; Issarawat Tattong/Moment; garysludden/E+; Roland Magnusson/EyeEm; Gary John Norman/The Image bank; Tim UR/iStock/Getty Images Plus; Artem Shevchenko/iStock/Getty Images Plus; art159/iStock/Getty Images Plus; ValuaVitaly/iStock/Getty Images Plus; RusN/iStock/Getty Images Plus; AnthiaCumming/E+; 2happy/iStock/Getty Images Plus; **U12:** Imgorthand/iStock/Getty Images Plus; Maskot; Gary John Norman/The Image bank; Tanes Ngamsom/iStock/Getty Images Plus; ATU Images/The Image Bank; hamurishi/iStock/Getty Images Plus; Alex Cao/Photodisc; Wong Sze Fei/EyeEm; Science Photo Library; BURCU ATALAY TANKUT/Moment; Greg Chapel/EyeEm; Eduardo Gonzalez Diaz/EyeEm; Patrik Giardino/Stone; Rebecca Nelson/DigitalVision; Sean Gallagher/National Geographic Image Collection; Stefan Cristian Cioata/Moment; Prasit photo/Moment; Natalia Rüdisüli/EyeEm; Hyoung Chang/Denver Post; AFP; bubaone/DigitalVision Vectors; TongSur/DigitalVision Vectors; -VICTOR-/DigitalVision Vectors; Westend61; andresr/E+; 2011 Dorann Weber/Moment Open; Stockbyte; malerapaso/iStock/Getty Images Plus; omada/iStock/Getty Images Plus; nevodka/iStock/Getty Images Plus; Tasakorn Kongmoon/EyeEm; jockermax/iStock/Getty Images Plus; aldomurillo/iStock/Getty Images Plus; Peerasak Kamngoen/EyeEm; Tanchic/iStock/Getty Images Plus; Roc Canals/Moment. vectorplusb/iStock/Getty Images Plus; DavidZydd/iStock/Getty Images Plus.

The following photos are sourced from other libraries.

U9: iprachenko/Shutterstock; Ronald Sumners/Shutterstock; **U11:** Sergei Kolesnikov/Shutterstock; iprachenko/Shutterstock; **U12:** MaraZe/Shutterstock; Wavebreak Media ltd/Alamy Stock Photo.

Commissioned photography by Copy cat and Trevor Clifford Photography.

Illustrations

Blooberry (source Pronk); Copy cat; Beatrice Costamagna, (Pickled ink); Chris Jones; Helen Naylor, (Plum Pudding); Kelly Kennedy, (Sylvie Poggio); Melanie Sharp, (Sylvie Poggio); Richard Hoit, Beehive; Xian Xio, (Illustrationweb); Beth Hughes (The Bright Agency); Clara Soriano (The Bright Agency); Dan Crisp (The Bright Agency); Gaby Zermeno; Jake McDonald (The Bright Agency); Matthew Scott (The Bright Agency); Pronk Media Inc.

Cover illustration by Pronk Media Inc.

Video

Video acknowledgements are in the Teacher Resources on Cambridge One.

Audio

Audio production by Creative Listening.

Design and typeset

Blooberry Design

Additional authors

Katy Kelly: Monty's Sounds and Spelling; Rebecca Legros: Marie's maths, art, geography, sports, and science; Montse Watkin: Exam folder.

Freelance editor: Pippa Mayfield

Contents

Hello again!

1 **Write the words.**

I'm Stella.

I'm Simon.

I'm Suzy.

Hello, I'm Grandma Star. This is my family.

She's ___Stella___ . He's _____ .

I'm Mr Star.

I'm Mrs Star.

I'm Grandpa Star.

2 **Write and draw.**

What's your name?

_____

How old are you?

_____

Me!

4   **Vocabulary:** character names   ⬚ Do the online activities on **Practice Extra** as you complete this unit

1 Colour the stars.

1 Colour two stars.

2 Colour five stars.

3 Colour six stars.

4 Colour one star.

5 Colour eight stars.

2 Match the questions and answers.

1	four + one =	7	eight
2	two + one =	5	seven
3	six + one =	8	five
4	eight + one =	6	ten
5	five + one =	9	six
6	seven + one =	10	three
7	nine + one =	3	nine

1 🎧 2 **Listen and colour. There is one example.**

t e b c d g p v

2 🎧 3 **Listen and point. Write the words.**

laelSt Szuy onmSi frou igteh sneev

1

This is ___Stella___ .
She's ___eight___ .

2

This is _____ .
He's _____ .

3

This is _____ .
She's _____ .

Vocabulary: the alphabet and colours | Language: greetings

Starters Listening

1 🎧 4 🐵 **Read the questions. Listen and write a name or a number. There are two examples.**

Examples

What is the boy's name?	Dan
How old is he?	9

Questions

1 What is the girl's name? _____

2 How old is the girl? _____

3 What is the name of Dan's street? _____ Street

4 What number is Dan's house? _____

5 What is the name of Grace's book? _____ House

monty's sounds and spelling

1 Complete the words. Look and say.

1 W h ere's the _____ ite _____ ale?
2 _____ ere's the red _____ ale?
3 _____ ere's the blue _____ ale?
4 _____ ere's the yellow _____ ale?

It's on the table.

2 Correct the words. Circle 'yes' or 'no'.

1 The blue walhe is under the train.   whale   **yes /** no
2 The red whale is next to the helew . _____ **yes / no**
3 The yellow hwael is in the bag. _____ **yes / no**
4 The wihte hwale is under the table. _____ **yes / no**

3 Ask and answer.   Can you spell 'whale'?   W-h-a-l-e.

My picture dictionary

1 🎧 5 **Listen and write. Stick.**

1 _purple_	2 _____	3 _____
4 _____	5 _____	6 _____

My progress

Tick or cross.

I can count to ten. ☐

I can say the colours. ☐

I can say the alphabet. ☐

2 Back to school

1 Find and write the words.

teacher

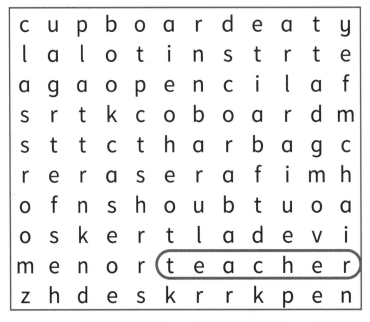

```
c u p b o a r d e a t y
l a l o t i n s t r t e
a g a o p e n c i l a f
s r t k c o b o a r d m
s t t c t h a r b a g c
r e r a s e r a f i m h
o f n s h o u b t u o a
o s k e r t l a d e v i
m e n o r (t e a c h e r)
z h d e s k r r k p e n
```

2 🎧 6 Listen and colour. There is one example.

📱 Do the online activities on Practice Extra as you complete this unit

Look and write the number.

veleen
11

niffeet
15

hiegeetn
18

eleven

ewletv
12

wytent
20

reihtnet
13

2 **Read and colour.**

17

19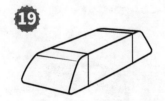

16

14

Colour number twelve brown.
Colour number nineteen pink.
Colour number fourteen green.
Colour number seventeen blue.
Colour number sixteen orange.

12

Make true sentences.

1 (a ruler) (There's) (the table.) (on)

There's a ruler on the table.

2 (the desk.) (There are) (on) (12 pencils)

_____

3 (There's) (under) (the chair.) (a bag)

_____

4 (the bookcase.) (16 books) (in) (There are)

_____

 Look at the picture. Answer the questions.

1 How many burgers are there?   There are six.

2 How many apples are there?   _____

3 How many oranges are there?   _____

4 How many cakes are there?   _____

5 How many ice creams are there?   _____

6 How many bananas are there?   _____

Language: *How many (books) are there? There's a (whiteboard). There are (11 desks).*

Starters Reading and Writing

1 **Look and read. Write 'yes' or 'no'.**

Examples

There are two teachers in the classroom. ....no........

There's a poster on the wall. ....yes........

Questions

1 There is a door next to the cupboard. ....

2 There is a board on the wall. ....

3 There are two tables under the board. ....

4 There is a ruler on a bookcase. ....

5 There are three cars under the desk. ....

Monty's sounds and spelling

1 **Complete the words. Draw.**

How many b____s
can you s____?

Sevent____n b____s
in the tr____.

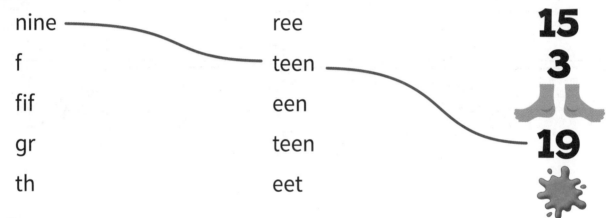

2 **Match and say.**

nine   ree   **15**

f   teen   **3**

fif   een

gr   teen   **19**

th   eet

3 **Find the sound. Draw a line.**

Start →

→ Finish

My picture dictionary

1 Complete the words. Stick.

taechre	baodr	rlure
teacher		
skde	bkoocsae	cpubaord

My progress

Tick or cross.

I can talk about my classroom. ☐

I can say the numbers 11–20. ☐

I can spell. ☐

Marie's maths

What do we use in our maths class?

1 🎧 7 **Listen and draw.**

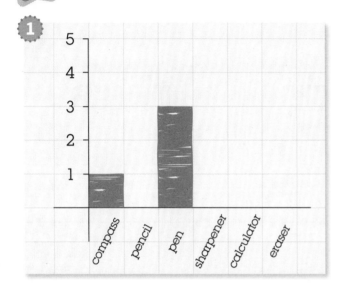

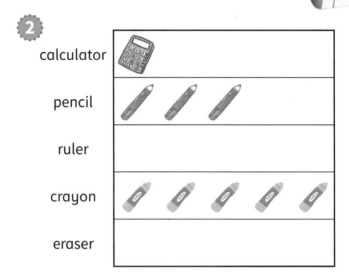

calculator

pencil

ruler

crayon

eraser

2 **Draw a bar chart or pictogram.**

3 Now you! **Ask and answer.**

(Is there a ... in your ...?)　(Yes, there is.)

Marie's maths | 🛡 critical thinking

Trevor's values

Be polite

Read and complete.

Can you   ~~come in~~   help you   Here's a   Is it   listen

1 Can we ___come in___, please?
Yes, come in.

2 I can _____ .
Thank you.

3 Yes, Dilek?
_____ a calculator?

4 I can _____ to my
teacher and my friends.
Very good!

5 _____ pencil.
Thank you.

6 _____ help me, please?
Yes, of course.

2 **Act out and say.**

3 Play time!

1 Read. Circle the toy words. Write.

k i t e

Suzy's got a (kite). Simon's got a robot.
Lenny's got a teddy bear.
Meera's got a board game.
Stella's got a tablet.
Alex's got a big yellow watch.

2 🎧 8 Listen. Tick a box.

1 a ✓   b   c
2 a   b   c
3 a   b   c
4 a   b   c

Make true sentences. Colour the toys.

1 __This__ is a red scooter.

2 __These__ are purple watches.

3 _____ are blue lorries.

4 _____ is a brown doll.

5 _____ are green tablets.

6 _____ are grey robots.

7 _____ are yellow cameras.

8 _____ are blue kites.

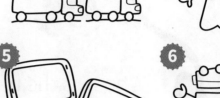

 Match and write.

k	kitchen	kite	ousers	obot
c	_____	_____	og	oll
r	_____	_____	ane	~~ite~~
d	_____	_____	ake	ease
tr	_____	_____	~~itchen~~	ain
pl	_____	_____	amera	uler

1 🎧 9 Listen and colour. Then answer.

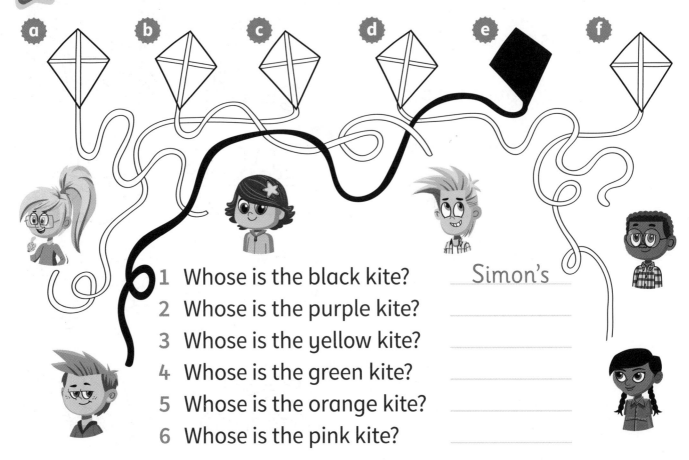

a   b   c   d   e   f

1 Whose is the black kite?   Simon's
2 Whose is the purple kite?   _____
3 Whose is the yellow kite?   _____
4 Whose is the green kite?   _____
5 Whose is the orange kite?   _____
6 Whose is the pink kite?   _____

2 Write the questions.

1 Whose is the kite?   It's Bill's.
2 _____   It's Lucy's.
3 _____   It's Ben's.
4 _____   It's Kim's.
5 _____   It's Nick's.

Language: *Whose is it? It's Stella's.*

Starters Reading and Writing

1 **Look and read. Put a tick or a cross in the box. There are two examples.**

Examples

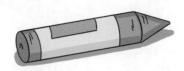 This is a ruler. [X]

 These are watches. [✓]

Questions

1   These are tablets. [ ]

2   This is a scooter. [ ]

3   This is a lorry. [ ]

4   These are aliens. [ ]

5   This is a robot. [ ]

Monty's sounds and spelling

1 **Look and write the words.**

| evfi | sitek | | tewih | kebi |

_____   _____   a _____   _____

2 **Look and write the words.**

There are _____

_____ in _____

_____ .

3 **Find and write the words.**

five

three

tree

kite

bee

bike

fourteen

nine

My picture dictionary

1 🎧 10 **Listen and write. Stick.**

1 _____kite_____	2 _____	3 _____
4 _____	5 _____	6 _____

My progress

Tick or cross.

I can talk about my favourite toy. ☐

I can write toy words. ☐

4 At home

1 🎧 11 Listen and draw lines. There is one example.

| Bill | Dan | Alice |

| Matt | | Eva |

| Pat | | Lucy |

2 Write the words. Find the secret word and draw.

	m	a¹	t		
			3		
				6	
		7	2		8
	4				
		5			

1 a	2	3	4	5	6	7	8

Me!

1 Read and write the number. Draw the furniture.

sixteen	=	16	→ m		twelve	=	_____	→ s
fourteen	=	_____	→ l		fifteen	=	_____	→ a
seventeen	=	_____	→ r		thirteen	=	_____	→ i
eighteen	=	_____	→ o		nineteen	=	_____	→ f
twenty	=	_____	→ p					

1

m					
16	13	17	17	18	17

Me!

2

14	15	16	20

3

12	18	19	15

2 Look and write the words.

mirror ~~bedroom~~ mat face bath

My bathroom is next to my (1) __bedroom__ . In my bathroom, I sit in the (2) _____ and wash my body. On the wall, there is a (3) _____ . You can see your (4) _____ in it. There is a blue (5) _____ on the floor. You can stand on it.

Write 'yours' or 'mine'.

1 Whose is this?

It's _mine_.

2 Is this _____ or Simon's?

It's mine.

3 Is this _____?

Yes, it is.

4 Whose are these?

They're _____.

2 🎧 12 **Listen and colour. There is one example.**

Language: *It's mine. It's yours.*

1 🎧 13 🐵 **Listen and draw lines. There is one example.**

Mark   Sue   Kim   Grace

Nick   Hugo   Matt

Monty's sounds and spelling

1 **Write and draw.**

sWohe   soen

_____ is this _____?

It's _____ 's

_____ !

2 **Write the questions.**

ears   mouth   nose   eyes

1 _____ is this  _____?

2 _____ are these _____?

3 _____ is this _____?

4 _____ are these _____?

3 **Ask and answer.**

Whose is this mouth?   Stella's!

My picture dictionary

1 **Complete the words. Stick.**

1 s o f a	2 m _ _ t	3 cl _ _ ck
4 ph _ _ n _	5 m _ rr _ r	6 l _ mp

My progress

Tick or cross.

I can talk about my house. ☐

I can say what's mine. ☐

Marie's art

What can you do with origami?

1 🎧 14 **What can Hiro make? Listen and tick.**

 ✓

 ☐

 ☐

 ☐

 ☐

2 **Fold, colour and write.**

1

2

3

4

5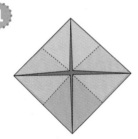

6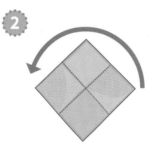

7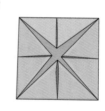
How old are you?

8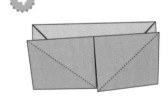
11 13 17 18 16

3 Now you! **Play the game.**

Red!   R-e-d!   Eleven!   1, 2, 3 ...   How old ...?

Trevor's values

Reuse and recycle

 1 Look, read and match.

1  **2**  **3**  **4**

a old jeans   **b** an old sock   **c** old paper   **d** a plastic bottle

 2 Draw a robot. You've got:

- four boxes
- two socks
- a T-shirt
- five pencils

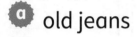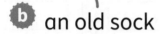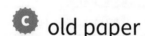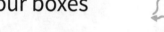

Review Units 1, 2, 3 and 4

1 Look, read and match.

7 grey	nine	8 yellow	three	5 pink
6 blue	ten	two	10 orange	four
five	3 purple	9 green	eight	1 brown
2 red	seven	six	4 black	one

2 🎧 15 Listen and write the number.

13

1 Write the questions. Answer the questions.

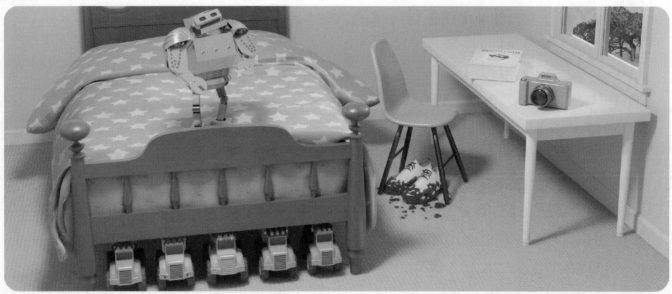

	a	b	c	d	e	f
1	what	lorries	dirty	how	big	bed
2	shoes	toy	clean	small	balls	whose
3	is	small	camera	many	are	chair
4	there	under	where	on	the	or

1 4c 3e 4e 1b
<u>Where are the lorries</u> ?
_____ .

2 2f 2b 3a 4d 4e 1f
_____ ?
_____ .

3 3e 4e 2a 2c 4f 1c
_____ ?
_____ .

4 1d 3d 1b 3e 4a
_____ ?
_____ .

5 4c 3a 4e 3c
_____ ?
_____ .

6 1a 3a 4d 4e 3f
_____ ?
_____ .

5 Meet my family

1 Read and write the names.

This is Lenny and his family. He's with his brother Sam, his sister May, and his cousin Frank. Lenny's brother has got a big nose. Lenny has got big eyes. Lenny's cousin is young. He's a baby. Lenny's sister has got long hair.

2 Write the words.

~~sofa~~   ~~mum~~   ~~plane~~   ~~bookcase~~   teacher   grandma   baby
kite   desk   lorry   grandpa   playground   cousin   bath   robot
board   mirror   boat   lamp   dad   bed   ruler   doll   phone

In the house	Family	Toys	At school
sofa	mum	plane	bookcase

Vocabulary 1: character names | Vocabulary 2: family

Do the online activities on **Practice Extra** as you complete this unit.

Read and write the name. Colour.

Hello. This is my family. My mum's got long purple hair, small green ears and five yellow teeth. Her name's Trudy. My dad's name's Tom. He's got short red hair and a dirty green nose. He's got eight brown teeth. My brother Tony's got long brown hair, big red eyes and one white tooth. My sister's name is Tricia. She's very clean! She's got big ears, short blue hair, orange eyes and six green teeth.

 Write the words.

bbya   afntharedrg   anthmoredrg   oremth

sstire   fthrea   dda   csinou   rthbore   mmu

 baby

baby

1 🎧 16 **Listen and write the number.**

 2 **Look at the pictures and write the letters.**

1 – What are you doing, Mum?
– I'm making a cake.

2 – Whose kite are you flying, Simon?
– I'm flying your kite, Suzy.

3 – What are you eating, Dad?
– I'm eating chocolate ice cream.

4 – Whose shoes are you cleaning, Grandpa?
– I'm cleaning Simon's shoes.

5 – Which word are you spelling, Stella?
– I'm spelling 'beautiful'.

6 – Who are you drawing, Grandma?
– I'm drawing Stella.

c
d
☐
☐
☐
☐
☐
☐
☐
☐
☐
☐

Starters Listening

1 🎧 17 🐵 **Listen and tick the box. There is one example.**

What is Dan doing?

1 Which girl is Anna?

2 What is Sue doing?

3 What is Grandpa doing?

4 What is Sam drawing?

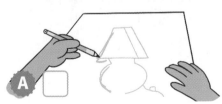   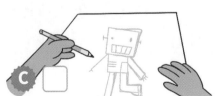

monty's sounds and spelling

 Write the words.

tac   colkc   ccroildoe

_____   _____   _____

 Look and write the words. There is one example.

The ___cat___ 's   The _____ 's   The _____ 's   The _____ 's
got a _____ .   k _____ a ball.   c _____   got a _____ .
                                  a _____ .

 Ask and answer.   Can you spell 'kicking'?   K-i-c-k-i-n-g.

My picture dictionary

1 🎧 18 **Listen and write. Stick.**

1 grandma	2 _____	3 _____
4 _____	5 _____	6 _____

My progress

Tick or cross.

I can talk about my family. ☐

I can talk about actions. ☐

6 Dinner time

1 Read and draw lines. Play the game.

Draw lines with a pencil.   Draw lines with a pen.

A

Shopping list

oranges
bread
rice
bananas
apples
milk
ice cream
burgers
apple juice
eggs
water

B

Shopping list

potatoes
rice
bread
carrots
fish
orange juice
chips
chicken
lemons
meat

Start

Start

Finish

Finish

Vocabulary: food   Do the online activities on **Practice Extra** as you complete this unit

1 Colour the food.

Colour the pears green.
Colour the carrots orange.
Colour the tomatoes red.

Colour the chicken brown.
Colour the meat red.
Colour the lemons yellow.

2 Draw and write about your favourite food. Ask and answer.

Me!

What's your favourite food for dinner?

It's chicken, chips and salad.

My favourite food is _____

 **19 Listen and circle the tick or cross.**

1

✓ (X)

2

✓ X

3

✓ X

4

✓ X

 Read and write the number.

a

Here you are. ☐

Can I have some juice, please? [1]

Orange juice, please. ☐

Which juice – orange juice or apple juice? ☐

b

Which fruit – a banana, a pear or an apple? ☐

Here you are. ☐

Can I have some fruit, please? ☐

A pear, please. ☐

Language: *Can I have some (bread), please? Here you are.*

Starters Reading and Writing

1 Read and choose a word from the box. Write the word next to numbers 1–5. There is one example.

My breakfast

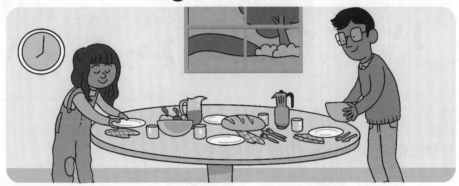

I eat my breakfast in the ___kitchen___ . I sit on a (1) _____ at the table. My dad and my (2) _____ sit with me. My favourite drink for breakfast is (3) _____ and I eat an (4) _____ with lots of bread. I don't like fruit. My dad loves fruit and he has two (5) _____ every morning for his breakfast.

Example

kitchen   egg   bananas   lunch

mirrors   chair   brother   milk

Monty's sounds and spelling

1 **Circle and write.**

chipslunchchickenchocolatecheese

chips _____

2 **Complete the words. Draw.**

The ___ildren
are wat ___ing TV
on ___airs in
the kit ___en.

3 **Find and write the words. Circle the 'ch', 'c', 'ck' and 'k'.**

chocolate

kitchen

chicken

crocodile

ch	c	k
chocolate	chocolate	
	ck	

kite
bike
kiwi

cheese
chips
lunch
clock

1 **Complete the words. Stick.**

ckinehc	gegs	pchis
chicken		
lkmi	rcie	dearb

My progress

Tick or cross.

I can talk about my favourite food. ☐

I can talk about breakfast, lunch and dinner. ☐

I can ask and answer questions about food. ☐

Marie's science

Where does food come from?

1 🎧 20 **Listen and write the number. Write 'plants' or 'animals'.**

 a ☐

 b ☐

 c ☐

 d 1

_____   _____   _____   _____

2 **Read and complete. Act it out.**

carrot   cheese   ~~chips~~   meat   pasta   potato   yoghurt

Lunch Menu

 fish and ^{1} _chips_

 ^{2} _____ and tomato ^{3} _____

 ^{4} _____ and ^{5} _____ noodles

 chicken and ^{6} _____ pie

 chocolate cake

 strawberry ^{7} _____

 ice cream

 orange juice

Can I have fish and chips, please?   Here you are.

3 Now you! **Play the game.**

My favourite food comes from an animal.   It's meat!   No.

Trevor's values

Eat good food

1 **Draw your favourite food.**

| milk   bread   eggs   juice   chicken   rice   water   fish |
| carrots   apples   meatballs   potatoes   bananas   oranges |

for breakfast   for lunch   for dinner

2 **Ask your friend. Draw your friend's favourite food.**

What's your favourite food for breakfast?

I like oranges and apples.

for breakfast   for lunch   for dinner

7 At the farm

1 Find and write the words.

```
w  a  l  e  r  s  d  s  p  i
s  h  e  e  p  t  u  p  l  d
e  d  m  e  y  k  c  i  r  a
p  m  i  u  s  a  k  d  b  y
t  h  c  h  i  c  k  e  n  a
e  w  t  o  g  o  y  r  o  b
c  a  s  r  z  w  i  l  s  i
h  f  i  s  h  e  t  r  h  r
a  r  t  e  l  i  z  a  r  d
m  o  u  s  e  f  r  e  n  d
s  g  o  a  t  r  f  r  e  v
```

horse

2 Read, draw and write.

~~snakes~~   ~~crocodiles~~   fish   lizards   bugs   giraffes   tigers   monkeys

This is the Star Zoo. The bugs are next to the snakes. The fish are under the bugs. The lizards are between the fish and the monkeys. The yellow and brown animals next to the monkeys are giraffes. The big orange and black cats under the crocodiles are tigers.

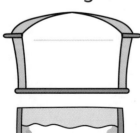

snakes

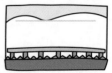

crocodiles

Vocabulary: animals   Do the online activities on Practice Extra as you complete this unit

1 Draw lines.

Ask your friend. Draw lines.

Where is the donkey? It's in the cupboard.

1 🎧 21 **Write the words. Listen and check.**

~~love~~   I   So   do   I   love   lizards   don't

1
a I __love__ spiders.
b So do _____.

2
c _____ love donkeys.
d _____ do I.

3
e I love _____.
f So _____ I.

4
g I _____ goats.
h I _____.

2 **Draw your favourite animal and write.**

Ask your friend.

What's your favourite animal?

Me!

I love _____.

50   **Language:** *I love* (lizards). *So do I. / I don't.*

Starters Listening

1 🎧 22 Listen and colour. There is one example.

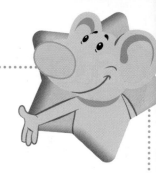

 1 **Look and write the words. There is one example. Match and write.**

k e n a s

i n a l s

p i d s r e

snake _____

_____

_____

w s o l

e y e d s p

r a c y s

a _____

b _____

c _____

 2 **Draw and write.**

_____

_____

3 **Ask and answer.** Can you spell 'slow'? s-l-o-w.

My picture dictionary

1 🎧 23 **Listen and write. Stick.**

1 spider	2 _____	3 _____
4 _____	5 _____	6 _____

My progress

Tick or cross.

I can write animal words. ☐

I can talk about things I love. ☐

8 My town

1 **Look and read. Tick or cross the box.**

1 This is a flat. ☒

2 These are boots. ☐

3 This is a hospital. ☐

4 This is a street. ☐

5 This is a park. ☐

6 This is a café. ☐

2 **Circle the different word.**

1 van	lorry	bus	(boot)
2 flat	town	goat	street
3 alien	café	hospital	school
4 kitchen	bedroom	bathroom	park
5 shop	cupboard	armchair	sofa
6 street	park	school	bedroom
7 bugs	hospital	café	flat
8 door	lion	window	floor

▶ Do the online activities on **Practice Extra** as you complete this unit

Spot the differences.

In A ___there's one car___ , but in B ___there are two cars___ .

In A _____ , but in B _____ .

In A _____ , but in B _____ .

In A _____ , but in B _____ .

In A _____ , but in B _____ .

In A _____ , but in B _____ .

 Write the words.

~~skateboard~~   ~~pear~~   ~~chair~~   ~~dog~~   coconut   armchair   table   bike
apple   alien   lizard   pineapple   cat   train   car   lemon
lorry   fish   mouse   mirror   clock   orange   bird   cupboard

FRAN's FRUIT
pear
_____
_____
_____

TED'S TOYS
skateboard
_____
_____
_____

Paula's PETS
dog
_____
_____
_____

PHIL'S FURNITURE
chair
_____
_____
_____

1 🎧 24 Listen and colour the stars. There is one example.

1　2　3

4　5　6

7　8　9

2 Read and write the names.

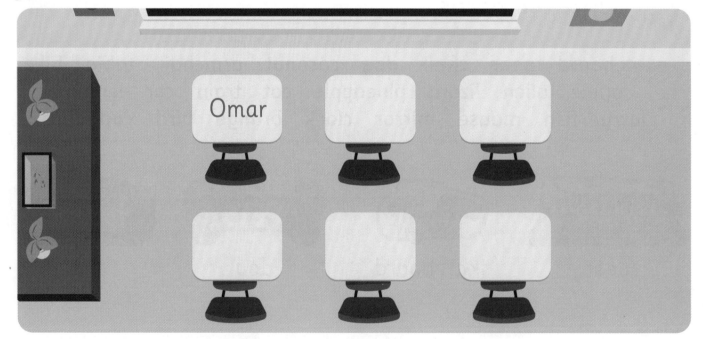

You're Omar. You're sitting in front of Jill.
You're Wendy. You're sitting between Omar and Nick.
You're Bill. You're sitting behind Nick.
You're Sue. You're sitting between Jill and Bill.

Starters Reading and Writing

1 🐵 **Look at the pictures and read the questions.
Write one-word answers.**

Examples

Where are the people?   at a ___café___

How many children are there?   ___two___

Questions

1 Where is the dog?   under the _____

2 What has the boy got?   an _____

3 What is the dog doing?   _____

4 Who is sad?   the _____

5 What is the dog doing now?   _____ the ice cream

monty's sounds and spelling

1 Circle and write.

grandpa pandajumppineapplehippopark

grandpa _____ _____

_____ _____

2 Look and write the words. There is one example.

1 The _____hippo_____ is in front of the _____ .
2 The _____ bike is behind a _____ .
3 The _____ is between the trees .
4 The pet _____ is next to the park.

3 Ask and answer.

It's next to the park.   The pet shop?   Yes!

My picture dictionary

1 **Complete the words. Stick.**

1 fl a t	2 p __ rk	3 sh __ p
4 h __ sp __ t __ l	5 str __ __ __ t	6 c __ f __

My progress

Tick or cross.

I can talk about the town. ☐

I can write about the town. ☐

Marie's geography

Where do we live?

1 🎧 25 **Listen and circle the tick or cross.**

1 Rory lives in a city.   ✓ (X)
2 Wendy lives in a flat. ✓ X
3 Rory loves cows.   ✓ X

4 Wendy is buying some books.   ✓ X
5 There's a hospital in Rory's village. ✓ X
6 There's a library on Wendy's street. ✓ X

2 **Look and write 'village', 'town' or 'city'.**

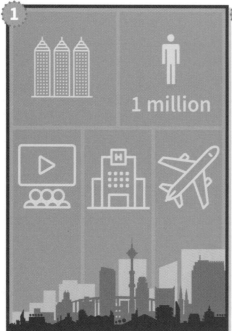

1 — 1 million

2 — 2,000

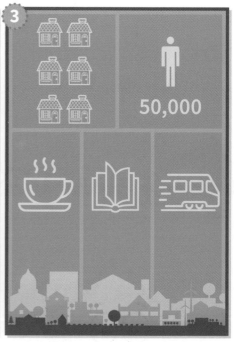

3 — 50,000

3 Now you! **Ask and answer.**   Is there a library in our …?

Trevor's values

Be responsible in your town

1 **Read and circle.**

1 There's a **red** / **green** man. You can cross the road.

2 Don't ride your skateboard **on the road** / **at the park**.

3 The sign says: **Don't walk** / **Walk** on the grass.

4 Put your **rubbish** / **books** in the bin.

5 We **wait** / **don't wait** in line here.

6 Stop! **There's** / **There isn't** a car! Don't cross the road!

2 **Look and write 'can' or 'can't'.**

I __can__ put my rubbish here.

I _____ walk here.

I _____ cross the road now.

I _____ play football here.

I _____ cross the road here.

I _____ wait in line for the bus.

1 Find and write the words.

food words
milk

t	g	f	r	u	i	t	x	d	j	u
b	r	e	a	k	f	a	s	t	u	w
r	a	a	m	u	m	g	y	c	i	g
o	n	w	n	m	c	j	x	h	c	h
t	d	a	d	d	t	o	s	i	e	e
h	m	s	l	o	i	i	i	p	k	d
e	o	p	a	b	h	k	s	s	s	i
r	t	m	i	l	k	t	s	m	n	
o	h	c	k	s	o	i	e	m	g	n
o	e	g	g	s	j	u	r	x	k	e
g	r	a	n	d	f	a	t	h	e	r

family words
brother

2 🎧 26 Listen and write the number.

1

1 Read and draw lines.

The baby is behind the door.
The mother is between the bed and the desk.
The clock is on the bookcase, between the books.
The cup is on the desk.
The polar bear is on the floor, in front of the bookcase.
There's a lion on the bed.

2 🎧 27 Listen and say the chant. Write the words.

> Whose   Which   ~~Who~~   What   How many
> Where   who   How old   What

1 __Who__ is that?
   That's my brother, Paul.

2 _____'s he doing?
   He's catching a ball.

3 _____ ball is it?
   It's my cousin Nick's.

4 _____ is he?
   He's very young.
   He's only six.

5 _____ is he now?
   He's in the hall.

6 _____'s he doing?
   He's throwing his ball.

7 _____ balls have you got?
   I don't know!
   We've got a lot.

8 _____ one's your favourite – red or blue?
   I don't know!

9 And _____ are you?

9 Our clothes

1 🎧 28 **Listen and join the dots.**

2 **Follow the 'clothes' words.**

watch	coat	glasses	lizard	cake
thing	frog	socks	burger	sheep
hat	T-shirt	jeans	carrots	goat
trousers	ice cream	cow	bread	spider
cap	skirt	jacket	shirt	handbag

How many clothes words are there? _____
Write the animal words. _____
Write the food words. _____

Vocabulary: clothes   📱 Do the online activities on **Practice Extra** as you complete this unit

1 Write the words. Colour the picture.

9

a	b	c	d	e	f	g	h	i	j	k	l	m
☆	■	○	▭	◆	◧	●	★	◆	△	▼	◡	◖

n	o	p	q	r	s	t	u	v	w	x	y	z
◣	☆	◤	◇	▲	◡	▽	□	▬	◗	▽	▭	◹

◆'◖/◡◡◆☆▲◆△●/■◡◡□◆/△◆☆▲◡,/☆/
I'm/ _____ / _____ / _____ ,/ ___ /

■◆◡◡☆◡/◡★◆▲▽,/●▲◆■□/
_____ / _____ ,/ _____ /

◡☆○▽◡,/■◡◡☆○▽/◡★☆◆◡/
_____ ,/ _____ / _____ /

☆▲▭□/☆/▲●◆◡◡/▲◆▭□/★☆▽.
___ / ___ / _____ / _____ / _____ .

2 Write about your clothes.

Me!

I'm wearing _____

_____

_____

_____

1 Look and write the words. There is one example.

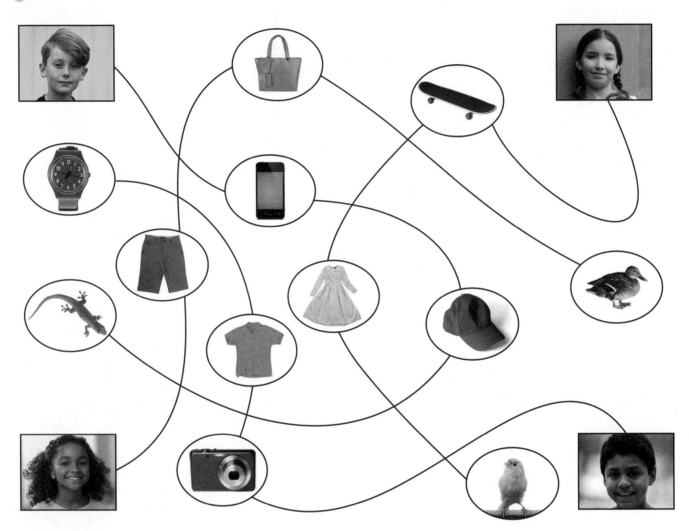

 I've got a black phone, a red baseball cap and a green lizard .

 I've got

 I've got

 I've got

Starters Reading and Writing

1  **Look at the pictures. Look at the letters. Write the words.**

Example

T - s h i r t

t h i s r T

Questions

1 _____

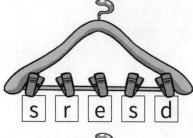

s r e s d

2 _____

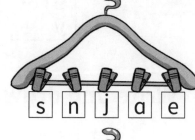

s n j a e

3 _____

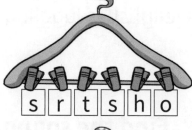

s r t s h o

4 _____

s s s l e g a

5 _____

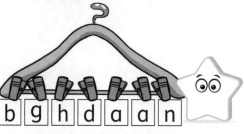

b g h d a a n

monty's sounds and spelling

1 Find and write the words.

jellyfish

b	a	s	j	u	g	e	r	n	a	l
d	k	u	i	b	e	d	j	v	j	x
a	q	d	a	h	a	i	f	n	e	a
j	o	r	s	x	e	v	o	w	l	n
u	i	e	f	i	g	u	b	j	l	m
i	d	r	j	e	a	n	s	n	y	i
c	u	m	a	l	e	v	k	e	f	s
e	z	f	c	g	c	q	d	p	i	o
f	o	n	k	z	x	y	c	r	s	p
y	u	w	e	l	p	o	w	s	h	t
v	e	r	t	v	c	o	u	l	m	k

2 Write and draw.

The jellyfish is juggling _____ _____ .

3 Find the sound. Draw lines.

Start →

→ Finish

My picture dictionary

1 🎧 29 **Listen and write. Stick.**

1 handbag	2 _____	3 _____
4 _____	5 _____	6 _____

My progress

Tick or cross.

I can talk about my clothes. ☐

I can talk about things I have got. ☐

1 Write the words. Look and write the number.

ptingain   painting   [4]

btonadmin _____ ☐

hokeyc _____ ☐

ktisdogareban _____ ☐

tleab nisten _____ ☐

ebbasall _____ ☐

2 🎧 30 Listen and colour. There is one example.

Write the words.

Down ↓   Across →

 Complete the sentences.

1 ↓ They're ___playing___ ___table tennis___ .
4 → They're _____ .
5 ↓ She's _____ .
6 → They're _____ _____ .
7 → She's _____ .
9 → He's _____ .

 **1** 🎧 31 **Listen and tick or cross.**

1 **a** ✓ **b** ✓ **c** ☐

2 **a** ☐ **b** ☐ **c** ☐

3 **a** ☐ **b** ☐ **c** ☐

4 **a** ☐ **b** ☐ **c** ☐

 2 **Draw and write about you.**

My name's _____.

I'm _____ years old.

My hair is _____.

My eyes are _____.

My favourite toy is _____.

I like _____.

I don't like _____.

I love _____.

My favourite hobby is _____.

Me!

72 **Language:** *I like / love / don't like (painting).*

Starters Reading and Writing

1 Look and read. Write 'yes' or 'no'.

Examples

Two boys are playing hockey.	yes
A girl is playing tennis.	no

Questions

1 A boy is wearing a black T-shirt. _____

2 Two boys are playing table tennis. _____

3 A tall girl is playing basketball. _____

4 The boy under the tree is reading. _____

5 A girl in a white skirt is playing badminton. _____

Monty's sounds and spelling

1 **Write the words.**

(lapy)

1 _____

(oatdy)

2 _____

(helaw)

3 _____

(sebbalal)

4 _____

(nilas)

5 _____

2 **Correct the words. Write the sentences.**

1 The whail loves paynting . The whale _____

2 The snale is plaing a gaym . _____

3 Let's plai hockey todai . _____

4 Pandas love baisball . _____

3 **Circle the words. Draw.**

(face)whalepaintingsnailbaseball

Sounds and spelling: *a–e*, *ai* and *ay*

My picture dictionary

1 **Complete the words. Stick.**

bdanimtno	tbale tneins	bsaeblal
badminton	_____	_____
bakstebllα	pniatngi	oeyckh
_____	_____	_____

My progress

Tick or cross.

I can write sport and hobby words. ☐

I can talk about my likes. ☐

Marie's sports

What sports can we do in summer and winter?

1 🎧 32 **Listen and tick or cross. Say.**

1

goggles ☐
snowboard ☐
wetsuit ☐
helmet ☐

2

snorkel ☐
wetsuit ☐
mask ☐
skis ☐

3

life jacket ☐
helmet ☐
trousers ☐
boat ☐

2 **Read and match.**

> My name's Molly and I'm from Australia. You can do lots of sports in the summer and winter here.

1 I've got a surfboard and a wetsuit.
2 I'm wearing a life jacket.
3 I've got a wetsuit and a mask.
4 I wear boots and I can do this in summer or winter.
5 I've got a helmet and skis.

a snorkelling
b skiing
c surfing
d sailing
e mountain walking

3 Now you! **Look and say.**

> I'd like to try skiing.

Marie's sports | 🛡 critical thinking

Trevor's values

Follow the rules

 Look and tick or cross the rule.

You can hit the ball with your head. ☐

You can catch the ball with your hand. ☐

You can kick the ball. ☐

You can throw the ball. ☐

You can't kick the ball. ☐

You can use a ball. ☐

 🎧 33 **Listen and say the sport.** It's hockey.

11 My birthday

1 Write the letters. Write the words.

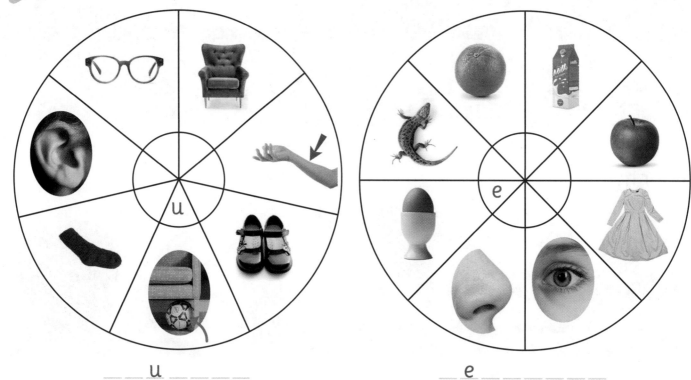

__ __ __ u __ __ __   __ __ e __ __ __ __

2 Circle the different word.

1	tree	garden	flower	(jug)
2	shoe	camera	robot	kite
3	sausage	armchair	pie	fruit
4	lemonade	salad	milk	water
5	badminton	basketball	soccer	watermelon
6	café	cake	hospital	school
7	cupboard	bed	sofa	kitchen
8	kitchen	hall	bathroom	skateboard

Vocabulary : food   📱 Do the online activities on **Practice Extra** as you complete this unit

 🎧 34 **Listen and draw.**

a   b   c   d

2 **Write the words.**

me you her it us ~~them~~

1
Look at ___them___ .

2
Can I play with _____ ?

3
Smile at _____ .

4
Take a photo of _____ .

5
Come and play with _____ .

6
Take a photo of _____ .

1 Make true sentences.

1 (fries?) (some) (Would) (like) (you)

Would you like some fries?

2 (some) (please.) (cake,) (like) (I'd)

_____

3 (Would) (like) (you) (to play) (us?) (with)

_____

4 (to play) (I'd) (table tennis.) (like)

_____

2 Read and complete.

Name	Food	Drink	Game
May	chicken and chips		
		water	
Ben			
			badminton

It's Anna's birthday and she's having lunch with her three friends, May, Ben and Sam.

1 May would like some chicken and chips and she'd like some orange juice.

2 Ben would like some meatballs and potatoes.

3 One boy would like some sausages and tomatoes, and he'd like some water.

4 Two children would like some lemonade.

5 The two boys would like to play hockey and the two girls would like to play badminton.

6 One girl would like some carrots and rice. It's her birthday today.

Language: *Would you like (some sausages)? Yes, please. No, thank you.*

Starters Listening

1 🎧 35 😃 **Listen and draw lines. There is one example.**

Tom   Jill   Dan   May

Mark   Hugo   Kim

Monty's sounds and spelling

1 Complete the words.

1 b___ger   2 b___d   3 p___ple   4 b___thday

2 Write the words. Draw and colour.

purple   girl   circus   burger   bird   skirt

1 A purple _____'s eating cake in the _____!
2 A _____'s eating a _____ on a bike!
3 A birthday girl's wearing a _____ _____!

3 Find the sound. Draw lines.

Start →

→ Finish

My picture dictionary

1 🎧 36 **Listen and write. Stick.**

1 _____cake_____	2 _____	3 _____
4 _____	5 _____	6 _____

My progress

Tick or cross.

I can ask for food and drink. ☐

I can talk about party food. ☐

12 On holiday!

1 🎧 37 **Listen and tick a box. Find the words.**

1 sea ✓   she ☐
2 song ☐   sun ☐
3 sand ☐   hand ☐
4 shell ☐   she ☐
5 mountain ☐   mouth ☐
6 three ☐   tree ☐
7 floors ☐   flowers ☐
8 bird ☐   big ☐
9 animals ☐   apples ☐
10 phone ☐   fish ☐
11 holiday ☐   today ☐

a	s	m	o	b	s	a	n	r
f	h	o	l	i	d	a	y	h
l	e	u	t	r	e	n	g	m
o	l	n	i	d	f	i	s	h
w	l	t	s	u	n	m	e	t
e	m	a	g	s	e	a	f	r
r	u	i	h	k	h	l	o	e
s	a	n	d	a	r	s	t	e

2 Match and write.

h	hockey	holiday	ountain	oliday
b			ell	ees
m			ockey	and
s			ouse	un
sh			ain	each
tr			eautiful	irt

Vocabulary: the world around us   ▶ Do the online activities on **Practice Extra** as you complete this unit

Answer the questions.

1 How many people are there? <u>There are four people.</u>
2 What's the man drinking? _____
3 What's the woman doing? _____
4 Is the dog walking? _____
5 Where's the boy swimming? _____
6 What's the girl picking up? _____
7 How many birds are there? _____
8 Where's the jellyfish? _____

2 Write the words.

1

dnas

sand

2

leshl

_____

3

leyljhifs

_____

4

chaeb

_____

5

erte

_____

6

nanitomu

_____

1 🎧 38 Listen and tick the box.

1 What does Nick want to do?

 a
 b ✓
 c

2 What does Mary want to have for lunch?

 a
 b
 c

3 What does Peter want for his birthday?

 a
 b
 c

4 What does Susan want to drink?

 a
 b
 c

5 What does Sally want to play?

 a
 b
 c

6 Where does John want to go?

 a
 b
 c

2 Read. Write 'Yes, he does' or 'No, he doesn't'.

> **Yousef's birthday list**
> A cool skateboard   A new kite
> A grey robot   A long ruler
> A small camera   A chocolate cake

1 Does Yousef want a cool skateboard?   _Yes, he does._

2 Does Yousef want a short ruler? _____

3 Does Yousef want a small kite? _____

4 Does Yousef want a grey robot? _____

5 Does Yousef want a small camera? _____

6 Does Yousef want some chocolate ice cream? _____

Starters Listening

1 🎧 39 🐵 **Listen and colour. There is one example.**

Monty's sounds and spelling

 1 Complete the rhyme.
Draw one picture.

A p u r ple ___at
with a k _ t ___ in a tr___

And a c h i ___en
p___nting a ___ale

A hi___o with a ___ider
on its no___

And a ___ellyfish
pl___ing with a sn___l!

 2 Write about the picture.

A girl's flying a purple kite.

_____

_____

_____

_____

_____

_____

3 Ask and answer.

What's the hippo doing?

My picture dictionary

1 **Complete the words. Stick.**

1 b e a ch	2 sh __ ll	3 s __ n
4 m __ __ nt __ __ n	5 s __ nd	6 s __ __

My progress

Tick or cross.

I can talk about my holidays. ☐

I can talk about what I want. ☐

marie's geography

Where do you want to explore?

 1 **Read and complete.**

STAR MAGAZINE   Young Explorers

Jordan Romero

Jordan's American. He climbs ¹ ⛰ mountains with his dad.

He wears a ² ⛑ _____, warm clothes and ³ 👢 _____ .

Jordan and his dad sleep in a ⁴ ⛺ _____ . They take

a ⁵ 🔦 _____ and ⁶ 🪢 _____ .

2 🎧 40 **Listen and write. Read and write 'yes' or 'no'.**

STAR MAGAZINE

Young Explorers

Name: Laura _____
Explores: the _____
Travels: on a _____
Age: _____

1 Laura Dekker explores the sea. _____

2 She flies a plane. _____

3 She takes a life jacket. _____

4 She looks at a map. _____

5 She wears a helmet. _____

 3 Now you! **Ask and answer. Write a list.**

(Where do you want to explore?)   (I want to explore …)

I need _____

_____ and _____ .

Trevor's values

Help on holiday

1 41 **Listen and write the number.**

a

b

1

c

d

2 **Write and draw.**

Me!

1 🎧 42 **Listen and join the dots.**

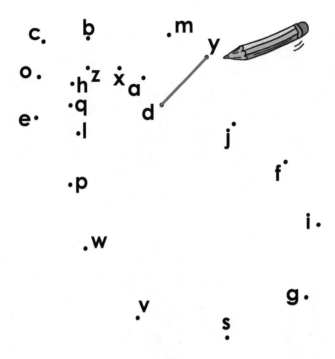

c.   ḅ   .m
                    .y
o.   .z ẋ
     .h   a.
e.   .q   d.
     .l

          .p

                    j.

                         f.

                              i.

     .w

          .v
               g.
          ṣ

What's this? It's a _____.

2 🎧 43 **Listen and colour. There is one example.**

Match the questions and answers.

1 Whose shorts are they? ☐ f
2 Where are they playing badminton? ☐
3 Who's that? ☐
4 What colour's your cup? ☐
5 What's Mr Star doing? ☐
6 Which coat is yours? ☐

a He's cooking.
b On the beach.
c The long, red one.
d It's green.
e She's my cousin.
f They're mine.

Read and complete.

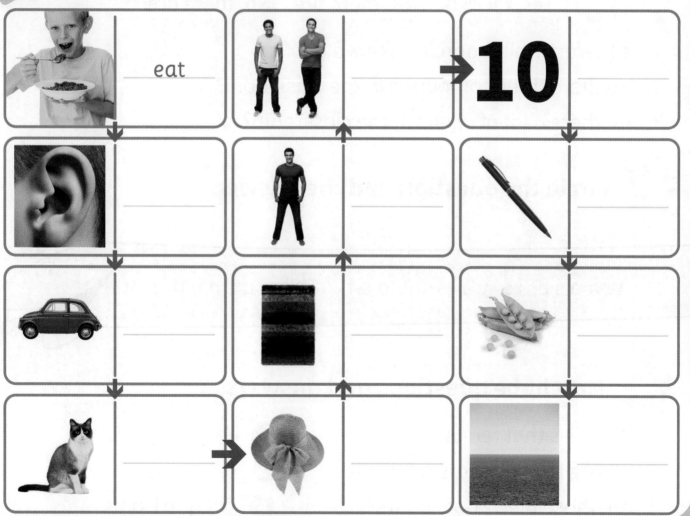

eat

→ 10

Grammar reference

1 **Make true sentences.**

1 (Chen) (What's) (his) (He's) (name)

_____ ? _____ .

2 (Who's) (She's) (Mrs) (Brown) (my) (teacher,) (she)

_____ ? _____ .

2 **Answer the questions.**

> Yes, there is   Yes, there are   No, there aren't

1 Is there a whiteboard on the wall? ✓ _____ .

2 Are there three computers in the classroom? ✗ _____ .

3 Are there a lot of chairs in the classroom? ✓ _____ .

3 **Circle the question and the answer.**

Whose is this robot? It's Lenny's.

4 **Match the questions and answers.**

1 Whose is that red dress?   **a** Yes, they are.

2 Whose blue trousers are those?   **b** It's mine.

3 Are those blue boots yours?   **c** They're Dad's.

Read and complete.

> 'm not   'm   're   're not   's   's not

1 ✓ I _____ singing.
2 ✗ I _____ dancing.
3 ✓ You _____ reading.

4 ✗ He _____ running.
5 ✓ She _____ playing tennis.
6 ✗ We _____ painting.

 Circle the question and the answer.

 Can I have some fish, please? Here you are.

 Look and write.

> So do I.   I don't.   So do I.

1 I like rabbits. ☺ _____
2 I like donkeys. ☺ _____
3 I like spiders. ☹ _____

8 Complete the words.

1 Where's the café? It's **bhnide** _____ the school.
2 Where's the park? It's **ni ofrnt fo** _____ the hospital.
3 Where's the shop? It's **teewenb** _____ the park and the flats.

9 **Answer the questions.**

haven't   has   hasn't   have

1 Have you got a skateboard?   ✓ Yes, I _____ .
2 Has he got red shorts?   ✗ No, he _____ .
3 Has she got a blue bag?   ✓ Yes, she _____ .
4 Have you got grey boots?   ✗ No, I _____ .

 10 **Read and complete.**

love   don't like   likes   doesn't like

1 ♥ ♥ I _____ reading.
2 ♥ He _____ playing badminton.
3 ✖ She _____ singing.
4 ✖ I _____ cooking.

 11 **Answer the questions.**

No, thank you   Yes, please

1 Would you like some meatballs?   ✓ _____ .
2 Would you like some milk?   ✗ _____ .

 12 **Read and complete.**

I want to   I don't want to

1 ☺ _____ go to the beach.
2 ☹ _____ go to a big city.

Hello again! (page 9)

 Back to school (page 15)

 Play time! (page 23)

black

purple

yellow

green

pink

blue

At home (page 29)

 Meet my family (page 39)

 Dinner time (page 45)

At the farm (page 53)

 My town (page 59)

 Our clothes (page 69)

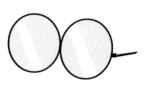

Our hobbies (page 75)

 My birthday (page 83)

 On holiday! (page 89)

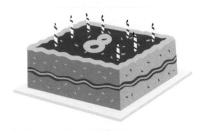